ISBN-13: 978-1518646096

ISBN-10: 1518646093

Dedicated to all who seek to
have life and have it abundantly.

Your Holiday Table

eat better. look better. feel better.

written by
Michelle Keyes

co-written by
Dr. Kevin Keyes, DC

photography by
Vincent T. Mims

Testimonials

eat better. look better. feel better.

Jill Donohue, Educator, Mom

The Keyes Ingredients Holiday Menu is a life-saver. While I enjoy cooking, I've always avoided hosting Thanksgiving dinner- too many different dishes that need to end up on the table at the exact same time. Too overwhelming. Last year we had friends come in from out of the country, so I thought I'd give it one more try. And thanks to the Keyes Ingredients Holiday Menu, it was a huge success! The recipes were simple- the kind that you read and think, "Ok... I can do that." Many of the dishes could be made in advance. I was able to enjoy Thanksgiving Day with my family because most of the dinner was already prepared. And the taste? Spectacular. The recipes use real food, not prepackaged products, so I felt good about serving the dinner. The end result was an outstanding meal that had everyone coming back for more!

Christy Nye, Integrative Nutrition Health Coach

Your holiday table will never look better. Not only is Michelle a genius when it comes to making healthy alternatives to those holiday recipes, but she's great at making it taste amazing as well. You won't want to pass on purchasing this book. She will make you look like a master chef over the holidays and you'll escape all the extra added holiday weight while enjoying your favorite recipes.

Dr. Robert Silverman, DC, MS, CNS, CSC S, CKTP, CES, CISN, DACBN, DCBCN, HICC, SASTM

Most people know I am very particular about what I eat. I always want to eat healthy and I need my ingredients to be wholesome. I had the opportunity to taste Michelle's thanksgiving meal and the food was fantastic. The ingredients she uses are beyond "A" plus. I just added her to the short list of people I will allow to cook for me. I am a fan and will definitely be getting a copy of this.

Table of Contents

Introduction

eat better. look better. feel better.

YOUR FOOD HAS CHANGED... Often times, I'm asked by the generations before me what the importance of organic ingredients is. The food that they ate was not labeled organic, non-GMO, or pesticide and antibiotic free, it just was. The foods eaten by generations before ours were made up of properly raised animals and crops grown in fertile soil. Food was made in the kitchen from those ingredients with love, not in a lab by food engineers. Our generation still has access to the food of our ancestors. Thanks to farmers, ranchers and fisherman with integrity, we are still able to feed our children the quality food that their grandparents ate when they were children. Better ingredients make better food, it can be proven in mineral and vitamin studies and with the taste buds of everyone around your table.

Food brings us together. As you gather around Your Holiday Table reflecting on the past year, you may laugh, you may cry, you may laugh until you cry or all of the above. As you join hands with family, friends and loved ones to give thanks, you will have the peace of mind to know that the food on your table will nourish your guests, heal the body and keep people coming back for seconds. These recipes are crafted with medicinal properties and proper balance in mind. They are formulated to reduce inflammation, balance blood sugar and with anti-cancer properties.

Welcome to our table! We're so glad you've joined us. As you raise your glass to celebrate life and the year that you've lived, have the confidence to know that you can change the way that your family is fed. The choices you make in the traditions that you keep will nourish your family for generations to come. Traditions have to start somewhere, why not at your holiday table?

Set a beautiful table, cherish your loved ones, and celebrate life!

Foreword

eat better. look better. feel better.

On a crisp fall day in Chicago of 2012, I embarked on a valued pilgrimage to the heat of San Antonio, Texas. I was going to an 8 Weeks to Wellness conference to connect, share and learn from some of the best Wellness Practitioners in the country. Little did I know that I would meet some of the best Texans on the planet who shared the same passion and mission for wellness, Dr. Kevin and Michelle Keyes.

Dr. Kevin presented at the conference, telling his story of how he transitioned from working in a Medical Clinic with over 100 MD's to starting one of the largest wellness offices in the Lone Star State. During his presentation he spoke of a life-altering event; their 3-year-old son Carson's battle with cancer and the struggle his family endured. I knew in that moment Dr. Kevin was not only a great doctor but a great human being. Behind every great man is a great woman, and that is Michelle Keyes.

I am Dr. Julie McLaughlin. With over 28 years of practice I am one of the most sought after wellness doctors in the Midwest. I teach celebrities, elite athletes, local entrepreneurs, business people, students and entire families how to create a healthy lifestyle that allows them to live, compete and perform at their highest level. This is achieved by harnessing the power of their body to move better, eat better, and think better. I have been called the "Doctor's Doctor" for mentoring doctors, chiropractors and their patients. I have not achieved these accolades on my own accord; just as I am a mentor to others, I too have been mentored.

Michelle Keyes has been my mentor when it comes to what to eat, when to eat, how much to eat, and most importantly why. You may be thinking that much of this is common knowledge, and it may well be, but it is not common practice. Michelle's website and this book are just a glimpse of the tools she has used to teach me how to better educate my patients about how to nourish their bodies with foods that have a purpose for healing. As you read this book and look at the beautiful photos, you will find a traditional holiday menu with foods that invoke memories of comfort, family and celebration. You will also discover special "Keyes Ingredients" that are secretly healing your body while you celebrate! Did you know Himalayan salt helps lower your blood pressure? Then there are the olive and coconut oils, the almonds, pumpkin, hemp and sesame seeds that give you monounsaturated heart protecting essential fatty acids. For the gluten-free crowd, you will find most of the recipes will work for you and give you the nutrients you need without the inflammation from unhealthy gluten protein. Once you experience the fresh ingredients, you will realize these truly are nature's healing foods. Michelle's Italian roots ensure none of the recipes lack flavor or beautiful presentation.

Your Holiday Table is a time for family, friends and gratitude. I am thankful for Michelle's passion to educate people about eating better. This fall Michelle will be educating some of the top Wellness Doctors in the country at an 8 Weeks to Wellness conference in Orlando, Florida. This makes a full circle from the initial time we met and her husband Kevin spoke. Michelle's dedication and knowledge for health are evident and poured into every recipe. Her gift as a nutrition educator, along with her strong instincts to keep her children healthy are the best combination for you to learn to do the same for your family. Enjoy the holidays knowing you are feeding your family only the very best!

Yours in Health,
Dr. Julie McLaughlin
Lake Bluff, Illinois

About this book

eat better. look better. feel better.

The question that I am asked most often is "Why?" Why do we need to read labels? Why do we need to buy quality ingredients? Why should we care how the cows and chickens we eat were raised? My answer is simple... eating better allows us to look and feel better.

Eat better

Eating better means to consume wholesome nutrient dense ingredients. It does not mean eating less or eating more. It does not mean eating fat free, sugar free or gluten free. Simply put, quality ingredients produce quality meals.

Look better

When our body receives the proper balance of macronutrients (carbohydrates, proteins and fats) in the right ratios, it knows where to put the fuel, burns fat more efficiently and builds health from the inside out. Our skin glows, our waistline shrinks and our confidence soars.

Feel better

By consuming healing ingredients we balance blood sugar, reduce inflammation and fight off chronic diseases such as diabetes, heart disease and cancer. We gain energy as our body becomes more efficient and begins to function at a higher level.

That is the reason I wrote this book. I want to share with you all that I have learned along the way. The healing power of food can be life changing, and what better time of year to come together with your family and begin that journey together.

Your Guide to Planning, Preparing, and Providing

eat better. look better. feel better.

Open your home and invite your loved ones to your holiday table. A traditional holiday meal is not usually created overnight just as Rome was not built in a day. The key to pulling off a successful and joyous holiday meal is to plan your menu in advance, prepare and freeze parts of the meal early and to know just what tasks need to be taken care of the night before or the day of. Investing the time into a well thought out plan and advance preparation will give you peace of mind knowing your family is being fed great food. You will be able to enjoy the festivities more because everything has already been done. If you have guests that want to contribute to the meal, delegate in advance and cross those tasks off your list. Be sure to purchase storage containers and label them with their contents. I use post-its and a sharpie marker. You can recycle the containers by sending your guests home with leftovers.

This simple 3-step plan will leave your guests wondering just how you pulled it all together while looking rested and still smiling! Your mood as a host and hostess sets the tone for your guests. Be thankful and enjoy the fruits of your labor.

Step 1:

Choose your Menu (2-3 appetizers, 1 soup, 1 salad, 1 main course, 1-2 types of stuffing, 2-3 colorful sides and your desserts)

Step 2:

Make your grocery list based on the recipes you chose. Delegate tasks in advance.

Step 3:

Follow your *E.A.T.* guide for preparing and providing a beautiful meal and environment for your family to come together and celebrate.

E = Early enough that you can freeze (2 weeks in advance)

- Crockpot oatmeal can be made early and frozen (all together or in 1/4 cup portions -I use a muffin tin)
- Pumpkin Pancakes can be made ahead and frozen. Use parchment paper between them and a toaster to heat them
- Cranberry Sauce (Jar and refrigerate)
- Spiced Olives (Refrigerate)
- Make cracker mix(es) and portion them into baggies (store in pantry)
- Stuffed Mushroom filling (freeze)
- Butternut Squash Soup (freeze)
- Butternut Squash Soup topping (can be frozen)
- French Onion Soup (freeze)
- Crockpot Mashed Potatoes (can be frozen)
- Pumpkin Pie (freeze)
- Apple Crumble (freeze)
- Brownie Bites (freeze-even with the raspberries on top)
- Pumpkin Pie Bites (freeze)
- Chocolate Cake (top with fresh fruit the day of)
- Frittata Muffins (freeze)
- Grainless Crunchy Granola (store in airtight container)
- Set your table and create your environment.

A = Advance (several days in advance)

- Fresh fruit parfaits can be made up to 48 hours ahead. Portion in 1/4 cup mason jars for small portions or in jam sized mason jars for larger portions, refrigerate
- Almond Bark (up to a week in advance)
- Roasted Nuts (up to a week in advance, store in airtight container)
- Bake crackers (3 days in advance, store in airtight container in pantry)...you may want to hide them
- Hummus (up to 5 days in advance)
- Roasted Eggplant Hummus (up to 5 days in advance)
- Touch of Maple Whipped Cream to top pies (1-2 days in advance)
- Prepare salad toppings (roast or candy nuts and store in airtight container)
- Thaw Stuffed Mushroom filling; stuff the mushrooms (1-2 days in advance)
- Leave bread out overnight for Bread Stuffing (3 days in advance)
- Bread Stuffing (2 days in advance and refrigerate)
- Quinoa Stuffing (2 days in advance and refrigerate)
- Marinate the turkey or chicken (2-3 days in advance, seal in a bag and refrigerate)
- Dry rub the Roast Beef (rub 3 days in advance, cover and refrigerate)
- Prep the vegetables for the roast (trim, cut, toss in olive oil, put in container and refrigerate)
- Crockpot Mashed Potatoes (refrigerate and add a little extra liquid when reheating - if frozen thaw now)
- Maple Sweet Potatoes (2-3 days in advance, cover and refrigerate)
- Cut veggies for medley, toss in oil and refrigerate
- Brussels can be trimmed and sauce made ahead and put in container (toppings can be made ahead of time and stored appropriately

- Roast and prepare Mashed Butternut Squash (1-2 days in advance)
- Green Beans Almondine (almonds can be roasted and stored in an airtight container)
- Thaw Chocolate Cake, needs to be refrigerated until serving (2 days in advance)
- Make the dressing for Festive Kale Salad (2-3 days in advance)
- Make the dressing for Candied Pecan, Pear and Arugula Salad (2-3 days in advance)
- Set your table if you have not already.

T= The night before or The day of entertaining

- Fill the mushroom caps for the stuffed mushrooms (the night before)
- Bake the Stuffed Mushrooms (the day of just before serving)
- Stuff and roast the turkey or chicken and follow roasting instructions (early the day of)
- Slow roast the beef (the night before or early the day of 6-8 hours of roasting required) Make the gravy as the roast and/or turkey comes out of the oven
- Thaw your soup - Butternut Squash or French Onion (the night before)
- Thaw Butternut Squash Soup topping (if you froze it)
- Set out and begin to warm the dishes you have already prepared
- Assemble the salads and prepare the soup toppings
- Festive Kale Salad (prepare pomegranate and nuts the night before, if not already done)
- Candied Pecan, Pear and Arugula Salad (prepare the nuts the night before, if not already done)
- Green beans can be trimmed (the night before) Frozen green beans are a time saver (the day of)
- Garlic Mint Peas (the day of)
- Roast vegetable medley (just before serving, the day of)
- Fresh Fruit Plate cut and put into containers the (night before), plate and serve (the day of)
- Caprese Skewers (secret is room temperature tomatoes) skewer other ingredients and put tomatoes on just before serving.
- Chocolate Covered Fruit (the night before)
- Crockpot Oatmeal (the night before serving), if frozen thaw now
- Eggs for a Crowd (can be prepped the night before and baked the day of)
- Frittata Muffins can be warmed up before serving (the morning of)
- Thaw pies, Apple Crumble, Pumpkin Pie Bites, Brownie Bites in the fridge the night before (set on counter the day of)
- Prepare your platters. Set out serving dishes, serving spoons, platters and bowls for everything you are serving. This way you won't find your un-served salad in the fridge the next day.

I truly hope this helps you put it all together. Remember, many hands make light work. Welcome the help and enjoy your day. Keep in mind that years from now no one will remember what you said or even how you said it. They will always remember the way you made them feel in your warm home and around your festive holiday table. Embrace your guests and enjoy celebrating life.

Until we eat again,
Michelle

appetizers

spiced olives – 14

caprese skewers – 16

maple pecan brie – 18

stuffed mushrooms – 20

hummus and crackers – 22

roasted eggplant hummus – 24

roasted nuts – 26

Spiced Olives

Ingredients

2 cups kalamata and/or green pimento stuffed olives

2-3 Tablespoons olive oil

1 teaspoon dried Italian spices

1 clove garlic, sliced

Instructions

1. Drain any brine or olive juice that the olives may be in

2. Put olives in separate bowl

3. Sprinkle spices, add the olive oil and garlic

4. Toss until coated

5. Put the olives back in the jar and allow them to marinate a few days for a stronger flavor

14

Caprese Skewers

Ingredients

20-30 small wooden skewers

20-30 small balls fresh mozzarella

20-30 grape tomatoes

1-2 packages fresh basil

1 cantaloupe melon made into 20-30 melon balls (optional)

20-30 kalamata olives or spiced olives

¼ cup olive oil

1 Tablespoon pesto

Instructions

1. Alternate the cheese, tomato, basil, melon and olives on the skewers in that order

2. Combine the olive oil and the pesto; drizzle over the skewers

3. Serve and watch them disappear

Maple Pecan Brie

Ingredients

Whole imported Brie cheese wheel

1/3 cup pecan halves

¼ cup pure maple syrup

Instructions

1. Preheat oven to 350 degrees

2. Place cheese wheel on an oven safe plate

3. Top with pecans and drizzle maple syrup

4. Bake for 10 min or until soft

Notes

Serve with "Carson's Crackers" and fresh fruit.

Apples, grapes and berries pair well also.

Stuffed Mushrooms

Ingredients

30 mushrooms, stem removed

½ cup Pecorino Romano cheese

½ cup feta cheese

½ cup cream cheese

3 Tablespoons Kalamata olives, minced

3 Tablespoons sun-dried tomatoes, minced

1 clove garlic, minced

¼ cup raw sunflower or pumpkin seeds, ground

3 Tablespoons kale, finely chopped

3 Tablespoons mixed colored bell peppers, finely chopped

2 Tablespoons fresh parsley, finely chopped

2 Tablespoons fresh basil, finely chopped

Instructions

1. Preheat oven to 350 degrees
2. Combine all ingredients except mushrooms in a bowl and mix well
3. Remove the stem of the mushrooms and push the mixture into the hollowed out centers
4. On a baking sheet lined with parchment paper, bake filled mushrooms for 15-20 minutes

Notes

Serve as an appetizer for any dinner party.

These accompany soups and salads very well.

If there is any filling mix left over, it can be frozen and used the next time.

Crackers

Ingredients

3 eggs

½ cup sunflower seeds

½ cup pumpkin seeds

¼ cup sesame seeds

¼ cup hemp seeds

¼ cup flax seeds

1 Tablespoon mixed dried Italian spices

½ teaspoon garlic powder

1 teaspoon pink Himalayan salt

Carson's Instructions

1. Preheat oven to 350 degrees

2. Combine eggs, seeds, spices, garlic powder and salt in a bowl; stir well

3. Use a spatula to transfer the mixture onto a cookie sheet lined with a silicone mat or parchment paper

4. Shake the cookie sheet and tilt it around until the mixture is spread across the cookie sheet

5. Bake for 10 minutes

6. Remove from oven and score with a pizza wheel

7. Put back in oven for 8-10 minutes or until crispy

8. Reduce oven temperature to warm (200 degrees) and allow to stand for 30-45 minutes

Isabella's Instructions

1. Preheat oven to 350 degrees

2. Combine all seeds and grind in a mill or food processor.

3. Combine eggs, seeds, spices, garlic powder and salt in a bowl; stir well

4. Use a spatula to transfer the mixture onto a cookie sheet lined with a silicone mat or parchment paper

5. Shake the cookie sheet and tilt it around until the mixture is spread across the cookie sheet

6. Bake for 10 minutes

7. Remove from oven and score with a pizza wheel

8. Put back in oven for 8-10 minutes or until crispy

9. Reduce oven temperature to warm (200 degrees) and allow to stand for 30-45 minutes

Hummus

Ingredients

2 (30 oz.) cans chickpeas

4 cloves garlic

4 Tablespoons tahini

Juice of 1 lemon

½ teaspoon pink Himalayan salt

¼ teaspoon pepper

Instructions

1. Rinse and drain chickpeas

2. Add to blender or Vita-mix

3. Add garlic, tahihi, lemon juice, salt and pepper

4. Blend until smooth

5. Spices and vegetables can be added to flavor the dip as you like. Ex: spinach, roasted red pepper, artichoke hearts or olives put a twist on this delicious hummus.

6. Serve with vegetables to dip or spread on Carson's Crackers

Roasted Eggplant Hummus

Ingredients

1 purple eggplant, cubed, skin on

¼ cup olive oil

¼ teaspoon pink Himalayan salt and pepper (more to taste)

¼ cup sesame seeds

4 cloves garlic, peeled (roasted with the eggplant for a milder garlic flavor)

Juice of 2 lemons

2 teaspoons cumin

¼ cup kalamata olives, diced (Spiced Olives recipe works great here)

2 Tablespoons fresh parsley, chopped

Instructions

1. Preheat oven to 450 degrees

2. Put cubed eggplant on a cookie sheet lined with parchment paper/baking mat. If roasting garlic add it to the eggplant

3. Drizzle olive oil over the eggplant, sprinkle with salt and pepper

4. Bake for 20 minutes or until golden brown

5. Remove and let cool

6. In a Vita-mix or blender, add the eggplant and all the olive oil that is on the parchment paper (you may have to use a spatula), sesame seeds, garlic if you did not already roast it), lemon juice, and cumin

7. Option: you can add ½ the olives to be blended or use them all for garnish

8. Blend until smooth

9. Use a spatula to transfer into a serving bowl

10. Garnish with fresh parsley and diced olives

Notes

The olives in this recipe are the "flavor", so they can be substituted with other popular Hummus flavors: roasted red pepper, spicy jalepeno etc.

This dip is served best with fresh colorful vegetables. It is wonderful spread on crackers or added to a sandwich or burger.

Roasted Nuts

Ingredients

2½ cups nuts

2 Tablespoons grass fed butter

1½ Tablespoons maple sugar

1 Tablespoon fresh rosemary, finely chopped

¼ teaspoon cayenne pepper

½ teaspoon pink Himalayan salt

Instructions

1. Preheat oven to 350 degrees

2. Melt the butter on the stove top and pour into large bowl

3. Add the maple sugar, rosemary, cayenne pepper and salt to the melted butter

4. Toss the nuts in the butter mixture

5. Spread on a cookie sheet and bake for 10 to 15 minutes

starters

butternut squash soup – 30

candied pecan salad – 32

french onion soup – 34

festive kale salad – 36

Butternut Squash Soup

Ingredients

The Soup

6 cups butternut squash, cubed

2 apples, quartered

1 large onion, quartered

2 shallots, finely quartered

2 carrots, chopped

4 leeks, chopped

1 clove garlic

12 cups of homemade chicken broth (unsalted)

2 teaspoons pink Himalayan salt (omit if broth is already salted)

2 Tablespoons coconut or olive oil

3 Tablespoons grass fed butter

½ cup heavy cream (optional for a richer soup)

The Topping

½ pound sautéed bacon (optional)

1 apple, diced

½ onion, diced

8 oz. mushrooms, finely chopped

A sprinkle of chives (fresh or dried)

Instructions

The Soup

1. Preheat the oven to 450 degrees

2. Peel the squash and cut into 1" cubes

3. Quarter apples, onions and shallots

4. Roughly chop carrots and leeks

5. Leave the garlic whole

6. Put squash, apples, onions, shallots, carrots, leeks
and garlic onto a cookie sheet lined with parchment paper

7. Toss with olive oil, salt and pepper

8. Bake for 15 to 20 min

9. Add chicken broth to a stockpot set on low to medium heat

10. Add roasted vegetables to the broth and simmer for 30 minutes

11. Purée in a food processor then return soup to the stockpot

12. Add the butter and simmer for 20 minutes

13. If adding cream, stir in toward the end of the simmer

14. Spoon prepared toppings onto soup before serving

The Topping

1. Prepare the bacon, onions, mushrooms and apples

2. Sauté in that order; cooking the bacon first and
adding the rest about 2-3 minutes after one another

3. Sauté until lightly browned

4. Add salt and pepper to taste

Candied Pecan And Pear Arugula Salad

Ingredients

Toasted Nuts

1 cup pecan halves (almonds or walnuts can be substituted)

1 Tablespoon butter

1 Tablespoon coconut sugar, maple sugar or maple syrup

The Dressing

½ cup olive oil

¼ cup tarragon vinegar

1½ teaspoons Dijon mustard

1 clove garlic, minced or leave whole and remove before serving

¼ teaspoon pink Himalayan salt

Optional: 1 sprig of fresh thyme (you will remove whole sprig before serving)

The Greens

5 cups butter lettuce, torn

5 cups arugula

2 cups chopped radicchio (optional) or use more butter lettuce and arugula

1-2 ripe red Anjou pears, thinly sliced

¼ -½ cup shaved Pecorino Romano (optional)

Instructions

1. Add nuts to a small saucepan set to low/medium heat and gently toast

2. Add butter and sugar

3. Stir until candied, being careful not to burn

4. Set aside

5. In a mason jar combine oil, vinegar, Dijon, garlic, salt & pepper and fresh sprig of thyme (optional)

6. Tighten lid and shake vigorously

7. In large bowl, combine lettuces and radicchio. Top with pear, cheese and candied nuts

8. In large bowl, combine lettuces and radicchio

9. Top with pear, cheese and candied nuts

10. If you added the sprig of thyme or whole garlic clove to the dressing, remove from the jar before serving

11. Drizzle dressing

12. Serve with additional cheese on the side

French Onion Soup

Ingredients

2-3 medium onions, halved and sliced thinly

2-3 sprigs fresh thyme

2 bay leaves

1 leek, sliced thinly

1 teaspoon pink Himalayan salt

¼ cup butter

1- 1½ cups red wine

6 quarts homemade beef broth

½ teaspoon pepper

Sprouted wheat bread croutons (optional)

8 oz. Gruyere or other imported Swiss cheese, grated

4 oz. Pecorino Romano cheese

Instructions

1. Sauté onions, thyme, bay leaves, leek and salt in butter in an uncovered 8 quart pot on moderate heat

2. Stir frequently until onions are very soft and deep golden brown, about 45 minutes

3. Stir in wine

4. Stir in broth, add pepper and simmer uncovered, stirring occasionally, 30 minutes

5. While soup simmers, put oven rack in middle position and preheat to 350 degrees

6. Portion the soup into bowls

7. Add the sprouted wheat croutons (optional) and cover the top with gruyere cheese and a sprinkle of pecorino romano

8. Put the bowls onto a cookie sheet and slide into the oven to melt the cheese; remove from oven when cheese becomes bubbly and gold

Notes

If you omit the croutons, cheese will sink into soup.

Festive Kale Salad

Ingredients

2 (20 oz.) bags kale, ribs removed, rinsed, drained and towel dried (spinach and/or other mixed greens can be substituted)

¼ red onion, sliced very thin

½ cup pecans (walnuts, almonds or a mix can be substituted)

½ cup shaved or grated Pecorino Romano

1 pomegranate, peeled and seeds separated

The Dressing

½ cup olive oil

¼ cup balsamic

¼ teaspoon pink Himalayan salt

2 teaspoons Dijon mustard

½ teaspoon maple syrup

Pepper to taste

Instructions

1. Place kale or spinach in salad bowl

2. Top with red onion, nuts, cheese and fruit

3. Add all dressing ingredients to a jar with a lid and shake until combined

4. Serve the dressing on the side or drizzle over salad and serve

the main stuff

slow roasted beef – 40

herb roasted chicken – 42

herb roasted turkey – 44

bread stuffing – 46

quinoa stuffing – 48

gravy – 50

Slow-Roasted Beef

Ingredients

Keyes Ingredients Spiced Dry Rub

1/8 cup Himalayan salt

1/8 cup mixed flax, sesame and hemp seed combined

1/4 cup paprika

1/2 teaspoon ground pepper

2 Tablespoons coconut sugar

1 teaspoon granulated garlic

2 Tablespoons Fresh herbs Rosemary, thyme and parsley (dried Italian spices can be substituted)

The Roast

Grass fed beef roast (your choice of cut, each will be tender)

2 cups beef broth or red wine

8-10 carrots, whole or halved

3 onions, peeled and quartered

Pink Himalayan salt and pepper to taste

Instructions

1. Preheat oven to 250 degrees

2. Rub the roast with olive oil and then with Keyes Ingredients Spiced Dry Rub 2 Tablespoons fresh herbs; rosemary, thyme and parsley (dried Italian spices can be substituted)

3. Roast can be refrigerated for up to five days if rubbed

4. In roasting pan on medium heat, sear both sides of roast in olive oil to crust the outside

5. Add beef broth or red wine to the pan

6. Arrange vegetables around the roast

7. Roast at 250 degrees 6 - 8 hours or cook in crockpot on low for 8 hours

8. Remove and allow to rest

9. Serve on a bed of fresh spinach or mixed greens of your choice

Herb Roasted Chicken

Ingredients

2 whole pasture raised chickens (3-5 pounds each)

½ cup olive oil

½ cup Dijon mustard

¼ cup tamari (organic soy sauce) or Braggs Aminos (soy sauce alternative)

1 cup mixed fresh herbs (parsley, sage, rosemary, thyme, chives), chopped

2-3 cloves of garlic, chopped

Juice of 4 lemons (1 cup)

Pink Himalayan salt and pepper to taste

4 onions, quartered

8-10 sweet/regular potatoes (optional, omit if serving mashed potatoes)

8-10 carrots

Instructions

1. Combine oil, mustard, tamari or Braggs Aminos, lemon juice, herbs and garlic

2. Mix thoroughly; pour into a large zippered or a turkey bag

3. Wash the chickens and remove innards

4. Put chickens in the marinade bag and marinate overnight or up to 48 hours

5. Preheat oven to 450 degrees

6. Place chickens in a roasting pan (I recommend cast iron)

7. Place breast side down and pour the marinade over them

8. Arrange the vegetables around the chickens

9. Top with salt and pepper to taste

10. Bake covered for 1½ hours or until meat thermometer reads 160 degrees and juices run clear

11. Remove lid to bronze up the bird for the last 10 to 15 minutes

Crock Pot Option

1. Put chicken and marinade into crockpot

2. Arrange vegetables around it

3. Add a little more marinade or white wine to the crockpot

4. Set on low and allow bird temperature to reach 160 degrees (a 4 lb. bird takes 6-8 hours on low depending on crockpot)

5. Remove from crockpot, place in a baking dish and place under the broiler for 5 minutes to bronze up

6. Remove and allow to rest

7. Carve and serve

Herb Roasted Turkey

Ingredients

1 whole good quality turkey (local farms are a good source)

1 cup olive oil

1 cup Dijon mustard

½ cup tamari (organic soy sauce) or Braggs Aminos (soy sauce alternative)

Juice of 8 lemons (2 cups)

2 cups mixed fresh herbs (parsley, sage, rosemary, thyme, chives), chopped

4-6 cloves of garlic, chopped

Pink Himalayan salt and pepper to taste

Instructions

1. Combine oil, mustard, tamari or Braggs Aminos, lemon juice, herbs and garlic, salt and pepper. Mix well and pour into a turkey bag

2. Wash the turkey and remove innards

3. Put into the marinade bag

4. Marinate overnight or up to 48 hours

5. Preheat oven to 450 degrees

6. Place turkey in a roasting pan (I recommend cast iron). Place breast side down and pour the marinade over top

7. Bake turkey at 450 for 15 minutes then reduce heat to 325 and roast accordingly

8. Check turkey halfway through. Once one side is bronze, flip to the other side

9. Turkey is done when the temperature with a meat thermometer is 180 degrees in thigh and 160 degrees in breast or stuffing

10. Lift turkey onto platter and let stand for 15 minutes before carving

Bread Stuffing

Ingredients

3 cups cubed sourdough, spelt or minimal ingredient artisan bread (that has been
left out over night to dry)

1 clove garlic, finely minced

1 onion, finely chopped

6-8 stalks celery, coarsely chopped

1 apple, skin on, cored and finely chopped

¼ cup cranberry sauce (see recipe)

2 Tablespoons parsley, finely chopped

2 Tablespoons rosemary, finely chopped

2 Tablespoons thyme, finely chopped

2 Tablespoons sage, finely chopped

¼ cup pine nuts, roasted

Juice of 1 lemon

Pink Himalayan salt and pepper

Instructions

1. Combine cubed bread, garlic, onion, celery, apple, cranberry sauce, fresh herbs, pine nuts and lemon juice in a large bowl

2. Add salt and pepper to taste

3. Refrigerate overnight; do not stuff into bird cavity until you are ready to bake

4. Wash and dry turkey and remove the innards

5. Spoon stuffing into turkey cavity and neck

6. Roasting times vary by weight for an unstuffed vs. stuffed bird, normally about 15 minutes per pound for an unstuffed turkey and 17 minutes per pound for stuffed

7. The stuffing can also be baked alone in a greased casserole at 350 degrees for 1 hour

Quinoa Stuffing (Grainless)

Ingredients

2 Tablespoons grass fed butter

1 Tablespoon olive oil

2 shallots, finely chopped

1 onion, finely chopped

6 ribs celery, finely chopped

1 clove garlic, minced

1 Tablespoon fresh parsley, finely chopped

1 Tablespoon fresh rosemary, finely chopped

1 Tablespoon fresh thyme, finely chopped

1 Tablespoon fresh sage, finely chopped

3 cups kale, finely chopped

2 cups chicken broth plus filtered water if stuffing gets dry when simmering

1 - 1½ cups quinoa (raw)

4 Tablespoons pine nuts, roasted

¼ cup cranberry sauce (dried cranberries can be substituted)

Instructions

1. In a medium sized skillet, add butter, olive oil, shallots, onion, celery, garlic, fresh herbs, and kale. Sauté 3-5 minutes

2. Add the chicken broth and quinoa. Simmer for 10 min

3. Remove from heat, add pine nuts and stir in cranberry sauce

4. Allow to cool

5. Wash and dry turkey. Remove the innards

6. Stuff into turkey cavity and neck

7. Roasting times vary by weight for an unstuffed vs. stuffed bird, normally about 15 minutes per pound for an unstuffed turkey and 17 minutes per pound for stuffed

8. The stuffing can also be baked in a greased casserole at 350 degrees for 1 hour

Beef Gravy

Ingredients

Roast drippings, strained

1 cup cold water

1-2 Tablespoons arrowroot flour

Pink Himalayan salt and pepper to taste

Splash of red wine (optional)

Instructions

1. Strain all the pan drippings from roast into a saucepan

2. Set on low to medium heat

3. Combine cold water with arrowroot flour in a mason jar, tighten lid and shake vigorously

4. Gently whisk water/flour mix into simmering beef drippings

5. Add salt, pepper and wine to taste

Poultry Gravy

Ingredients

Turkey or chicken drippings, strained

1 cup cold water

1-2 Tablespoons arrowroot flour

Pink Himalayan salt and pepper to taste

Instructions

1. Strain all the pan drippings from turkey into a saucepan

2. Set on low to medium heat

3. Combine cold water with arrowroot flour in a mason jar, tighten lid and shake vigorously

4. Gently whisk water/flour mix into simmering turkey drippings (if it is boiling it will clump)

5. Add salt and pepper to taste

sides

maple sweet potatoes – 54

garlic mint peas – 56

crockpot mashed potatoes – 58

green beans almondine – 60

mashed butternut squash – 62

brussels – 64

cranberry sauce – 66

vegetable medley – 68

Maple Sweet Potatoes

Ingredients

6 medium sweet potatoes (1½ to 2 pounds)

1 stick unsalted butter

1 cup pure maple syrup

Coarse pink Himalayan salt and freshly ground pepper

Instructions

1. Preheat oven to 400 degrees
2. Cut potatoes into 1 -1½ inch cubes
3. Melt butter in a large cast-iron or other ovenproof skillet over medium heat
4. Add sweet potatoes
5. Add maple syrup
6. Toss potatoes to coat and bring to a boil
7. Transfer skillet to oven
8. Cook, stirring occasionally, until potatoes are golden, well glazed, and tender when pierced with a fork, about 20 minutes
9. Remove from oven
10. Season with salt and pepper

Garlic Mint Peas

Ingredients

½ a shallot, minced

2-3 Tablespoons grass fed butter

1-2 cloves garlic, minced

1 bag frozen green peas

2 Tablespoons fresh mint leaves, finely chopped

Pink Himalayan salt and pepper to taste

Instructions

1. In small pan sauté the shallots in butter
2. Add in the garlic and stir
3. Add in the peas
4. Stir until warmed
5. Add fresh mint leaves
6. Salt and pepper to taste

Crockpot Mashed Potatoes

Ingredients

5 pounds organic potatoes with or without the peel

1½ cups homemade chicken broth

1 cup grass fed butter, cubed

1 Tablespoon pink Himalayan salt

2 cloves garlic, minced

1 teaspoon pepper

1½ cups milk

¼ cup sour cream (optional)

Fresh chives for garnish

Instructions

1. Place the potatoes, broth and butter into a 4-5 quart slow cooker

2. Season with salt, garlic and pepper

3. Cover and cook on high for 4 hours or until potatoes are fork tender

(Different types of potatoes have more or less starch so cooking time may vary. Set a timer and check consistency.)

4. Do not remove the excess liquid from crockpot - this adds to the creamy texture

5. Mash potatoes adding the desired amount of milk to achieve a creamy consistency

6. Check consistency and stir more butter and/or a ¼ cup sour cream in just before serving

7. Garnish with chives

Green Beans Almondine

Ingredients

3 pounds green beans, washed and ends removed

3 Tablespoons butter (plus 1 Tablespoon to toast almonds)

Pink Himalayan salt and pepper to taste

½ cup slivered almonds, toasted

Instructions

1. Bring large pot of water to boil

2. Add beans and boil for 9-12 minutes or until desired tenderness

3. Drain water. Toss beans in butter and season with salt and pepper

4. Toast slivered almonds in 1 Tablespoon butter and add to beans just before serving

Mashed Butternut Squash

Ingredients

2 butternut squash, peeled and cubed

1 onion, coarsely chopped

¼ cup olive oil

½ teaspoon pink Himalayan salt

1 Tablespoon grass fed butter

Instructions

1. Preheat oven to 450 degrees

2. Combine squash and onion

3. Toss with olive oil and sprinkle with salt

4. Bake for 20 minutes on cookie sheet lined with parchment paper

5. Remove and mash with a potato masher

6. Stir in butter and transfer to serving dish

Brussels

Ingredients

3 cups brussels, halved and trimmed

¼ onion, chopped

2-3 Tablespoons olive oil

¼ cup roasted pumpkin seeds

½ cup pancetta or bacon (optional)

¼ cup grass fed butter

2-3 Tablespoons white wine

½ teaspoon coconut sugar

2 Tablespoons Dijon mustard

Instructions

1. Preheat oven to 425 degrees

2. Toss brussels and onion in olive oil

3. Spread on a cookie sheet lined with parchment paper and roast for 20 minutes

4. While they are roasting, sauté pancetta or bacon until crispy and set aside

5. Combine butter, white wine, coconut sugar and mustard in a sauce pan

6. Stir and keep warm

7. Remove brussels from the oven

8. Roast pumpkin seeds in 350 degree oven for 10 minutes (if you have a toaster oven you can use that)

9. Coat brussels with sauce and top with bacon or pancetta and roasted pumpkin seeds

Cranberry Sauce

Ingredients

Two 12-ounce bags fresh cranberries

Juice of 3 large oranges

Juice of 1 lemon

2 cups pure maple syrup

2 Tablespoons zest from oranges and lemon

Instructions

1. In a saucepan combine fresh cranberries, juice from oranges, lemon, maple syrup and zest

2. Bring to a gentle boil

3. Simmer on low to medium heat for 20 minutes

4. Transfer to glass dish and refrigerate overnight

5. Can be made in advance and frozen as well

Vegetable Medley

Ingredients

1 butternut squash, peeled and cubed

1 head cauliflower, cut into florets

1 bunch asparagus, cut in thirds

1 red bell pepper, cut in squares

1 yellow bell pepper, cut in squares

1 zucchini, quartered and sliced

½ purple onion, sliced

½ white onion, sliced

¼ cup olive oil

Pink Himalayan salt and pepper to taste

Instructions

1. Preheat oven to 400 degrees
2. Prepare vegetables and combine them in a large bowl
3. Toss in olive oil and arrange on a cookie sheet lined with parchment paper
4. Sprinkle salt and pepper to taste
5. Bake for 20 minutes

Notes

Leftovers are great in omelets or as a side.

Toss this veggie medley with high protein pasta, olive oil, Pecorino Romano and fresh basil and you have pasta primavera!

desserts

brownie bites – 72

pumpkin pie – 74

chocolate cake – 76

pumpkin pie bites – 78

chocolate covered fruit/fruit platter – 80

apple crumble – 82

almond bark – 84

Brownie Bites

Ingredients

10 eggs

2½ cups cooked black beans (rinsed/drained)

2 teaspoons vanilla

2 teaspoons baking powder

1 teaspoon baking soda

1 cup raw cacao / cacao powder

1 cup coconut oil (in liquid form)

1 cup honey

Topping

2 Tablespoons grass fed butter

1 cup mini chocolate chips

Instructions

1. Preheat oven to 350 degrees

2. In a Vita-mix, food processor or large capacity blender, in the following order combine eggs, black beans, vanilla, baking powder, baking soda, cacao, coconut oil and honey (heat coconut oil and honey on low to ensure it is in liquid form)

3. Blend ingredients into a batter

4. Pour 1/8 cup of batter into each mini cupcake paper

5. Bake for 15-18 minutes

6. Check for doneness with a toothpick

7. Remove and allow to cool before serving

Chocolate Glaze Topping

1. Melt the butter and chocolate chips in a saucepan on low heat

2. Either dip the cooled bites in the melted chocolate or drizzle melted chocolate over the top

Notes

These are meant to be bite sized to avoid over-indulgence! Bake them in the mini sized tins.

Pumpkin Pie

Ingredients

2 cups pureed pumpkin (or substitute organic canned pumpkin)

¼ teaspoon nutmeg

1 teaspoon ginger

1 teaspoon cinnamon

2 Tablespoons grass fed butter, melted

2 small eggs (If using large use a little less)

1/3 cup maple syrup

½ cup coconut sugar

1 cup evaporated milk

2 Tablespoons coconut flour

½ teaspoon pink Himalayan salt

1 unbaked pie shell. Suggestion: If using a nut-based crust do not extend over the edge of pie plate, as it will burn quickly

Press crust into bottom and up the sides more like a torte

Instructions

1. Preheat oven to 425 degrees

2. In medium sized bowl, combine pumpkin and spices

3. Pour melted butter into pumpkin mix

4. In a separate bowl, beat eggs until frothy

5. Add maple syrup, coconut sugar, evaporated milk, coconut flour and salt to eggs

6. Gently combine the pumpkin mixture with the egg mixture and pour into pie shell

7. Bake for 10-15 minutes. Watch closely

8. Reduce heat to 350 degrees and bake for 30-35 minutes

9. Cool and serve or freeze

Nut N' Better Pie Crust

Ingredients

2½ cups ground pecans

¼ teaspoon ground cinnamon

1/3 cup coconut sugar

4 Tablespoons unsalted grass fed butter, melted

Instructions

1. Stir together ground nuts, cinnamon and sugar

2. Mix in melted butter

3. Press the mixture into the bottom and up the sides of a 9-inch, deep-dish style pie pan

4. Chill the unbaked crust in the refrigerator for about 30 to 45 minutes before filling

5. Fill crust with your choice of pumpkin pie or apple crumble filling

6. Place filled piecrust on a cookie sheet and position on the middle rack of oven

7. Bake according to filling instructions. WATCH the crust carefully, as nut crusts burn easily; they DON'T have to turn black to taste burnt!

Chocolate Cake

Ingredients

Bottom Layer

3 eggs (place in a bowl of warm water to bring to room temperature)

1/3 cup coconut sugar

1/3 cup almond flour

2 Tablespoons cacao

3 Tablespoons Grand Marnier or orange flavored liquor (optional)

Top Layer

½ cup coconut oil

½ cup butter

14 ounces good quality dark chocolate

¾ cup coffee

6 egg whites

¼ cup coconut sugar

Raspberry Coulis

8 ounces frozen raspberries

2 teaspoons fresh lemon juice

2 Tablespoons maple syrup

Instructions

1. Preheat oven to 350 degrees
2. Beat eggs and sugar together
3. Sift flour and cacao together and fold into egg mixture
4. Spread into 9 inch greased spring form pan
5. Bake for 12-15 minutes or until toothpick comes out clean
6. Allow to cool and brush the top with the orange liquor (optional)
7. In a saucepan on low heat melt the butter and coconut oil and stir together
8. Add the chocolate - watch carefully and continue to stir until completely blended
9. Pour the coffee into the chocolate mixture and stir well
10. Beat egg whites until they peak
11. Add the sugar to the egg whites and beat another 10-20 seconds
12. Fold chocolate and egg whites together
13. Pour onto cake base and refrigerate overnight
14. To make the coulis, simmer the raspberries, lemon juice and syrup for 4-5 minutes
15. Put through a sieve and decorate the dessert with this sweet surprise

Touch of Maple Whipped Cream

Ingredients

1 pint heavy cream

3 Tablespoons maple syrup

1 teaspoon vanilla

Instructions

1. Place bowl and beaters in freezer for 20-30 minutes to chill
2. Add cream to chilled bowl
3. Mix on high for 2-3 minutes
4. Add maple syrup and vanilla while whipping
5. Continue whipping until desired texture is achieved

Pumpkin Pie Bites

Ingredients

¼ cup organic butter

2 cups pumpkin puree

¼ cup pure maple syrup

2 Tablespoons coconut oil, melted

¼ teaspoon nutmeg

1 teaspoon cinnamon

1 teaspoon ground ginger

1 teaspoon vanilla

½ teaspoon pink Himalayan salt

6 pasture raised eggs, beaten

2 teaspoons baking soda

½ cup coconut flour

1 cup almond flour

Topping

6 Tablespoons pecans, chopped

6 Tablespoons pure maple syrup

2 Tablespoons coconut oil or butter

Instructions

1. Preheat oven to 325 degrees

2. In a saucepan on low heat melt butter

3. Add pumpkin, maple syrup, coconut oil, nutmeg, cinnamon, ginger, vanilla and salt

4. Stir about 10 minutes over low heat

5. Remove from heat and stir in eggs

6. In a separate bowl combine baking soda, coconut flour and almond flour

7. Add pumpkin puree mixture to flour mixture and stir to combine

8. Spoon into greased silicone mini muffin tin or mini cupcake papers

9. Combine pecans, maple syrup and coconut oil in a saucepan. Heat together on low and spoon a teaspoon of mixture on top of muffins

10. Bake for 20-30 minutes or until toothpick comes out clean

Notes

These are meant to be served as mini bites! Bake them in mini cupcake tins

Chocolate Covered Fruit

Ingredients

12 strawberries or cut up fruit(s) of your choice

3-4 ounces good quality ingredient dark chocolate (72% cacao or higher)

1 teaspoon coconut oil or butter

Instructions

1. Melt chocolate in 1 teaspoon coconut oil or butter in saucepan on low heat

2. Dip fruit pieces one at a time

3. Place on a plate lined with wax or parchment paper

4. Refrigerate until chocolate hardens

Fresh Fruit Plate

Ingredients

Melons

Organic strawberries

Pineapple

Oranges

Grapes

Fennel

Instructions

1. Cut up into desired sizes

2. Arrange beautifully on a plate

Apple Crumble

Ingredients

The Filling

4-6 medium sized organic apples, chopped

1 Tablespoon coconut sugar

1 Tablespoon lemon juice

½ teaspoon cinnamon

1 Tablespoon arrowroot powder

½ cup water

The Crumble

¼ cup ground pumpkin or sunflower seeds

½ cup almond flour

¼ cup coconut flour

2 Tablespoons coconut sugar

½ teaspoon cinnamon

¼ teaspoon pink Himalayan salt

1 teaspoon pure vanilla extract

2 Tablespoons grass fed butter, room temperature

Optional

This crumble pairs nicely with the Nut n' Better Crust

* A traditional or gluten free crust may also be used. You can also grease your pan and go crustless.

Instructions

1. Preheat oven to 350 degrees

2. In medium sized bowl combine chopped apples, coconut sugar, lemon juice, cinnamon and mix well

3. Put arrowroot flour in a jar and add the water. Shake until dissolved and pour over the apples

4. Transfer apples to greased pie plate baking dish, lotus parchment cups in a muffin tin or the nut n' better crust

5. In a separate bowl combine ground seeds, flours, coconut sugar, cinnamon, salt, vanilla and butter

6. Mix into a crumble and top the apples

7. Bake for 35-40 minutes or until apples are soft and crumble is golden

8. These can be done in individual portions as well if you use small cast iron or porcelain ramekins

Almond Bark

Ingredients

Basic Almond Bark

4 cups dark chocolate 72 percent or more cacao

4 Tablespoons grass-fed butter

2 cups whole almonds

¼ cup sliced almonds (reserve some to sprinkle on top)

¼ cup whole flax seed

¼ teaspoon pink Himalayan salt

Cranberry Pumpkin Bark

4 cups dark chocolate 72 percent or more cacao

4 Tablespoons grass-fed butter

¾ cup dried cranberries

1 cup raw pumpkin seeds (reserve some to sprinkle on top)

¼ cup whole flax seeds

¼ teaspoon pink Himalayan salt

Instructions

1. Melt butter in a cast iron pan on low heat

2. Add chocolate, stir until smooth

3. Add nuts and/or seeds and stir in until well mixed

4. Pour onto a cookie sheet lined with parchment paper

5. Sprinkle top with slivered almonds and/or pumpkin seeds

6. Refrigerate until solid

7. Break into pieces…make sure you grab a piece before it's gone

8. Using a chocolate mold increases that BAM factor!

breakfast

granola – 88

fresh fruit parfait – 90

eggs for a crowd – 92

crockpot oatmeal – 94

frittata muffins – 96

french toast casserole – 98

pumpkin pancakes – 100

Grainless Crunchy Granola

Ingredients

1½ cups nuts - almonds, pecans or mixed

4 cups unsweetened shredded coconut

1 cup pumpkin seeds

1 cup sunflower seeds

½ cup chia seeds

½ cup hemp seeds

1 cup sesame seeds

1 cup flax seeds

1 teaspoon pink Himalayan salt

½ cup virgin coconut oil or grass fed butter

½ cup raw honey or maple syrup

½ teaspoon cinnamon (optional)

Instructions

1. Preheat oven to 350 degrees

2. In a large bowl combine nuts, coconut, seeds and salt

3. In small saucepan on low liquefy the coconut oil and honey/maple syrup

4. Pour coconut oil/honey mixture over nut/seed mixture and stir until well combined

5. Spread onto cookie sheets covered in parchment paper (Do not overfill)

6. Bake for 15 minutes

7. Check and move around halfway through so outside granola does not overcook

8. Remove and let cool

9. Store in airtight containers

Fresh Fruit Parfait

Ingredients

4 ounces organic yogurt

1/2 teaspoon cinnamon

1/3 cup fresh berries

1/4 cup crunchy granola

Instructions

1. Stir cinnamon into yogurt

Layer yogurt, berries, granola and repeat until jar is full

Eggs for a Crowd

Ingredients

Coconut oil to grease muffin tin

12 farm fresh eggs

6 Tablespoons cream (coconut cream can be substituted for a dairy free option)

6 teaspoons fresh herbs (basil, dill, cilantro etc.)

12 teaspoons grated cheese (optional)

Pink Himalayan salt and pepper to taste

Instructions

1. Preheat oven to 350 degrees
2. Grease a muffin tin with coconut oil
3. Crack 1 egg into each muffin tin cup
4. Top with ½ teaspoon of cream, herb of choice, cheese and a sprinkle of salt & pepper
5. Bake for 10-12 minutes or to desired softness

Variations

The Italian: Tomatoes, mozzarella and fresh basil.

The Southwestern: Black beans, pepper jack and cilantro.

Serve with whole grain toast or a sprouted grain english muffin topped with cream cheese.

Sliced tomatoes drizzled with olive oil and sprinkled with salt and pepper is another great side.

Crockpot Oatmeal

Ingredients

1 Tablespoon coconut oil

2½ cups water

2½ cups whole milk (coconut milk may be substituted for a dairy free option)

½ cup cream (coconut milk may be substituted for a dairy free option)

1 cup steel cut oats

1 cup rolled oats

2 teaspoons vanilla

1/3 cup maple syrup

1½ teaspoons cinnamon

3 small apples of your choice, diced or grated

Instructions

1. Grease the crockpot with coconut oil

2. Combine water, milk, cream, oats, vanilla, maple syrup, cinnamon and apples in crockpot

3. Cook on low for 6 hours or high for 2 hours

Top With

½ cup chopped pecans

Drizzle of maple syrup and a dash of cinnamon

Feel free to get creative with this one and add another warming spice or some fresh fruits for the topping

Frittata Muffins

Ingredients

2 pounds grass fed ground beef

1 cup onion, finely chopped

2 Tablespoons butter

1 cup grape tomatoes, quartered

1 cup kale, spinach or arugula, finely chopped (fresh or frozen and drained)

1 bunch fresh cilantro, finely chopped

15 eggs, beaten

¼ cup water

Pink Himalayan salt and pepper to taste

2 Tablespoons sunflower seeds, ground

2 Tablespoons hemp seeds

Coconut oil or butter to grease silicone muffin pans

Mini or full size muffin pans

Instructions

1. Preheat oven to 350 degrees
2. Pan fry beef, season with salt and pepper, set aside
3. In a small frying pan, on low-medium heat sauté onions for 2-3 minutes in butter
4. Add tomatoes and sauté another 2-3 minutes
5. Stir in the spinach, kale or arugula
6. Turn the burner off and stir in the fresh cilantro
7. In separate bowl mix eggs, water and salt & pepper
8. Add the beef, seeds and vegetables to the egg mixture and stir well
9. Spoon into greased muffin tins until almost full
10. Bake for 25-30 minutes or until golden
11. Yields 24 muffins

French Toast Casserole

Ingredients

Coconut oil for baking dish

12 pieces sprouted grain cinnamon raisin bread, crusts removed

6 ounces organic cream cheese, softened

6 eggs, beaten

4-6 ounces of milk (non dairy substitutions may be made)

½ teaspoon cinnamon

1 Tablespoon vanilla

2 cups homemade granola for topping

Garnish with:

Organic yogurt

Maple syrup

Fresh fruit

Instructions

1. Grease a 9x13 glass baking dish with coconut oil
2. Spread each piece of bread with cream cheese
3. Arrange the bread in greased baking dish
4. Place second piece of bread on top of the first, cream cheese side up. There should be two layers.
5. Beat eggs, milk, cinnamon and vanilla together and pour over the bread
6. Cover and refrigerate overnight
7. In the morning, bake covered at 350 degrees for 30 minutes
8. Remove cover, spread granola over the top and bake loosely covered for another 10 minutes
9. Remove cover for a few more minutes to allow the granola to crisp up

Notes

Allow to cool, cut into squares and serve - yields 10 servings.

Top with a drizzle of yogurt, pure maple syrup, and fresh berries.

Pumpkin Pancakes

Ingredients

The Pumpkin part

2 cups pumpkin purée

¼ cup organic butter

¼ cup pure maple syrup

¼ teaspoon nutmeg

1 teaspoon cinnamon

1 teaspoon ginger

The Pancake part

3 eggs

1½ cups milk (cows, coconut or almond)

½ cup coconut oil, more for frying

1 Tablespoon vanilla

2 cups spelt flour

2 Tablespoons baking powder

½ teaspoon pink Himalayan salt

2 Tablespoons coconut sugar

Instructions

1. In a small saucepan mix pumpkin purée, butter, maple syrup, nutmeg, cinnamon and ginger together
2. Simmer about 5-10 minutes and set aside to cool
3. Separate eggs into 2 bowls
4. Put yolks in a medium size bowl and whip the whites in another
5. Add milk, liquefied coconut oil (run jar under hot water) and vanilla to egg yolks and set aside
6. In a separate bowl, mix spelt flour, baking powder salt and sugar together
7. Add dry ingredients to egg yolk mixture
8. Stir in cooled spiced pumpkin purée
9. Fold in egg whites
10. Use a ¼ cup measure to spoon into a 10-inch fry pan (3 at a time) in approximately 1 teaspoon of coconut oil
11. Flip when bubbles form for golden brown cakes
12. These freeze well

Epilogue

eat better. look better. feel better.

Big changes are easier to make by taking small steps. Some simple modifications in your diet will help start your journey to eating better, looking better and feeling better.

Replacing iodized table salt with pink Himalayan salt is one of those small changes that will make a big difference. Pink Himalayan salt can help your body balance pH, regulate water content, remove toxins, absorb nutrients, prevent muscle cramping and lower blood pressure.

Another change you can make is by removing refined sugar and replacing it with coconut sugar, which is lower on the glycemic index. Raw honey and pure maple syrup are also healthier sweeteners.

Swapping out enriched white flour and processed grains, which are stripped of vital nutrients, with smarter alternatives like coconut or almond flour are good choices because they are not only gluten free but also high in fiber and lower in carbohydrates. Ancient grains like organic spelt and kamut are also high in fiber, protein, vitamins and minerals.

Substituting artery-clogging hydrogenated oils with healthy fats such as coconut and olive oils, avocados, seeds and nuts will protect your heart and support overall health. The answer isn't cutting out the fat; it's learning to make healthy choices and to replace the bad fats with good ones that promote health and well-being.

These recipes incorporate the healthy alternatives mentioned above. They are designed to help make your holidays stress free and healthful. Many can be made ahead and frozen, eliminating the need to spend most of the day in the kitchen. There is nothing better than knowing that your holiday table is set with nutritious, delicious food that you prepared together. Enjoy!

Contributors

eat better. look better. feel better.

Dr. Kevin Keyes, DC - my dedicated husband for his love, support, and for always leading with integrity

Carson Keyes	Isabella Keyes
Charlie and Estelle Mula	Angela DeBellis
John and Marilyn Keyes	Kathryn Guthrie
Bridget Buck	Jenny Lipham
Christy Roeder	Tina Smith
Dr. Julie McLaughlin	Jill Donohue
Christy Nye	Dr. Robert Silverman
A'lisa Ghali	Valerie Lowry
Jason Lowry	Sandy Flowers
Vince Mims	Nicolo and Angelina Mula

A very special thank you to the Kramer Family of Yonderway Farms. It is Farmers like them that make it possible to eat better. Quality meat, the best eggs on the planet and hard core true work ethic. It sure is nice to shake that hand that feeds me.